T0209978

SECRETS TO A BETTER LIFE

TWENTY, THIRTY, FORTY

years old
...and counting

JOY A. SIMONS BROWN

BALBOA.PRESS
A DIVISION OF HAY HOUSE

Balboa Press books may be ordered through booksellers or by contacting:

Balboa Press
A Division of Hay House
1663 Liberty Drive
Bloomington, IN 47403
www.balboapress.com
1 (877) 407-4847

Scripture quotations are from New Revised Standard Version Bible, copyright © 1989 National Council of the Churches of Christ in the United States of America. Used by permission. All rights reserved worldwide.

Print information available on the last page.

ISBN: 978-1-9822-4187-2 (sc)
ISBN: 978-1-9822-4188-9 (e)

Balboa Press rev. date: 01/23/2020

Contents

Introduction

Although this book is dedicated to everyone who wants to live a better life, it specifically addresses the concerns of people between the ages of twenty and forty years old.

Why would I write a book for this age group?

Not too many years ago, I was part of this age group. I encountered many challenges, made many decisions, and wondered about many issues as they arose. After a number of years, I found myself asking, "Why isn't any information available to help me make these decisions?" "Did I hold on to things that I later learned were a waste of time?" or "Did I overlook anything that would have made my life better today?"

Now, my daughters and their friends are entering this age group and are facing similar issues that I faced. They, too, are just going along with life. If they understood the impact of their choices, then they would be more proactive, starting now.

The twenties are the time of life when you move from being dependent on parents and to now being responsible for yourself. It is a big shift. It is likely that you are coming from a place of feeling secure and now are faced with having to make your own decisions. Some choices you make may be based on the principles and examples to which you were exposed while growing up in your adolescent and teen years, some will be a rejection of those very same principles and examples, some might be decisions made based on what you have heard of or read about somewhere outside your family, and still other decisions might be made based on a fantasy you have always had.

I won't dare claim to know the answer to every issue you will face, but some challenges and decisions in this journey called life are common to most people; however, from one generation to the next, everyone seems to be reworking the decision-making process and "reinventing the wheel." This is because we engage in hardly any discussion and sharing of information, which would make life far less stressful for everyone.

The idea for this book arose out of a genuine need to share discoveries. It is like having a conversation with my twenty-year-old self and highlighting some of the main issues that need to be addressed to make life easier. Examples and anecdotes support various suggestions. Yes, that is exactly what they are, suggestions. My hope is that this information will enlighten you and open discussion on as many platforms as possible. Even if the exact answer for every individual question is not found among these pages, at least you will be made aware that many other people are trying to come to terms with similar issues.

This is my gift to you. Thank you for your interest. Please visit: www. twentythirtyforty.org join the discussion, and share this gift with someone else who may need it.

So, What Do You Say?

After putting together several drafts of this book, I decided to support and enrich the information by including the views held by the age-group being discussed. I contacted one hundred and twenty persons between twenty and forty-nine and asked them to do an informal survey. I sent fifty questions by email and they were asked to respond by email. Five persons found the questions 'too profound" and opted out but the rest, fifty-four males and sixty-one females, completed the survey. The intention was to get a general overview of their perceptions of life as it relates to age.

Many people have the same questions about life. The summary of results is presented as a list at the end of Chapter 16 Responses, and it should make for some interesting reading. You might want to have these questions in mind as you read through these chapters discussing the secrets of a better life. Here are the questions:

Age: Gender:

1. What do you love most about your life, now?
2. If you had the chance to relive your childhood up to age sixteen, what would you have done differently?
3. What are your best childhood memories (under ten years old)?
4. Looking ahead, what are your concerns?
5. Are you satisfied with your career choice?
6. Do you think you have enough fun in your life?
7. Do you find some of your beliefs lacking or unfulfilling?

8. What questions do you have about life?
9. What are the things you don't love about life, but that you have to accept?
10. What do you think is your life purpose?
11. What advice, about life, would you give to someone age fifteen?
12. What makes you truly happy?
13. What cause do you feel strongly about?
14. Do you worry about disasters? Sickness?
15. What is it that you see in people over sixty years old that you fear most?

1

THIS IS YOUR LIFE

It is interesting to follow the process of learning throughout your short life. After all, what you learned, saw, and experienced, we could say, defined your culture.

At first, you learned how to do all the basic things. You were encouraged to crawl, walk, talk, and identify and name objects, as you grew familiar with the world around you.

Then you learned similarities and differences between dogs and cats, up and down, and near and far, and soon you began to form your own opinion about all the new things you encountered.

Your parents or caregivers used smiles, frowns, the index finger, and the words "yes" and "no" to teach you right from wrong. You might even have received punishment with the intention of driving home, more forcefully, what was acceptable and what was not. Because they were bigger, spoke louder, paid the bills, and gave the orders, you (more or less) did what you were told to do and therefore opted for what seemed to be a peaceful life.

Later, outside your family, teachers, pastors, coaches, and extended family members also guided you. You developed a pretty good idea of what they all expected of you and the boundaries within which you were expected to operate.

Add to that your college tutors, your friends, and others around who might have had some influence on you. Also consider the daily reporting and persuasion delivered by the media. All these channels brought you to where you are today.

So, where are you now?

You have passed through your teen years and have celebrated one or two birthdays in your twenties or thirties or maybe even your forties. You might be single or married, with or without children. You might be employed or self-employed, or perhaps you are looking for a job. You might have traveled and have had many adult experiences. You may have developed your own views of love, life, freedom, abuse, money, and relationships, and you surely have formed opinions about yourself.

This might be the most interesting place in time that you ever will find yourself.

You might ask, "Why is this so?"

Well, childhood is long gone and you have many years ahead. You likely are physically removed from all those teachers of the past. You now are making your own decisions without consulting any of those mentors, but their values still may be a major influence your decision-making.

This is the point in your life when you can look back and objectively assess the worth of all the coaching you received, the mistakes you made, and the many things you, and you alone, know that you did. What about the risks, the secret embarrassments, the friends you have lost touch with, the new friends you have found, the illnesses, the losses, the achievements, the wishes unfulfilled, and all those things you thought were good for you?

This is the point in your life when you can look ahead, way down the road, and wonder how your own life will turn out. What changes will you make in your career, your relationships, or your health? You may ask, "Will I have enough money?" "Will my big dream come true?" or "What am I living for?"

Looking around at others you might feel that the course of life is a path of luck. After looking at people in similar situations with different results you may wonder, "Are there any rules?" The questions will keep coming: "How will I deal with loss, an unexpected disaster, and the many changes that are possible?" "Could I use the value system, the preferences, the rules that I was taught, to cope?" and "Are there any guarantees?"

You will see people thirty or forty years older than yourself, and some you will admire and some you won't. You'll wonder what choices they made. Some seem to cope and seem active and successful, whereas others seem to be just plodding along, barely surviving.

In truth, you cannot be certain about the future. The many changes ahead could be less traumatic, however, if you thought about them, talked about them, and learned lessons from other people's experiences.

For those you admire, you remember what they were like when you were just a child, and you wish they could give you a glimpse into the future and offer some advice. They could do this, of course, but whatever you do is still up to you.

3

We have considered where your values and your habits originated. Now you have a good idea of how you arrived at this point. Let us look at other issues and chart a probable future.

This is your life.

2

DON'T STOP LEARNING

We know that since we were born we have been learning. We ask ourselves, "Isn't school over?" "When is studying and knowing more, going to stop?" In this chapter, we try to identify a time when enough is enough. Is there such a time?

Mark: Lifelong learning

Mark was looking forward to his graduation from university in June. From as far back as he could remember, he never had been a bright student. He struggled with fractions, he had problems putting his thoughts on paper to make a sensible-sounding essay, and most of the time his best friend Andrew had to help him out with homework. His father, with his power voice, always reminded him, "Son, if you intend to get anywhere in life, you have to study. Nobody will ever hire someone who is underqualified, and no woman wants a husband who isn't able to work and take care of the family."

With his father's words and quiet encouragement from his mother, he struggled through high school, doing extra lessons to keep up, and university work continued to be stressful. He was happy now that all of this studying and lessons were over once and for all.

His happiness was short lived, however, when he soon had to face the fact that there was more to be done if he wanted to get ahead in the world.

Does this mean learning like schoolwork? Yes. Two types of learning must be done: (1) active intentional learning, which many people resist, and (2) learning by observation, which occurs in the course of daily living.

Look at the world today. Because of leaps in technology, procedures and methods continue to change exponentially. As computers become available in smaller and smaller units, users are able to make contact in real time and get quick answers using the thousands of applications that are being designed. It is a big mistake to believe that we can survive and move ahead with a limited understanding of technology. Access to the Internet has opened possibilities and vast information now is available with the click of a mouse. Online courses, online payment systems, and various social media platforms enable you to learn, conduct business, and introduce yourself to others all the while keeping up with the many technological changes. Many networks enable you to form relationships and facilitate business.

The mystery of video editing, use of illustration and design programs, and operation of all kinds of software are demonstrated free of cost. But you have to get online, use these technologies, and stay in the loop to get ahead. Marketing, in particular, and business, in general, both have emerged as new fields. You can learn to be savvy with world affairs and investment options right from your living room. New words are being added to everyday speech and methods of communication are being updated daily.

This might sound like encouragement to join the rat race. But, no, it is not. You can get involved in only what you choose. The most important thing to know is that the possibilities are endless. If you don't keep learning, you will get left behind in a world that constantly is moving forward.

In earlier years, people used to study toward attainment of a certain career and, whatever their dissatisfaction, they stuck with it until retirement. Now, there are no excuses. If opportunities present themselves for more learning that align with your interests, then find a way to go for it, whether or not you already have a job.

The second type of learning requires little or no effort and comes through observation. The child who used to open his hand to receive an allowance becomes the father or spouse who has to find the money to pay the bills. Some things that worked years ago no longer are applicable and something has to change. You form new relationships, discover new coping skills, and learn from mistakes. The concept of your place in the world will change and you have to seek information to move along with the times. As long as you are alive, you have to keep learning.

You can accommodate all these changes in several ways. You really have to become creative, be persistent, and roll with the punches.

Mark was shocked to know that although he left the physical classroom, he likely would continue learning and studying to achieve what he truly wanted in life. The good thing was that he could study what he truly enjoyed and pursue this information in his own time. He didn't have to feel stuck.

So, when does learning end? When will school be over? Never!

3

YOUR FIRST DUTY TO YOURSELF AND YOUR FAMILY

Yes, I hear you wondering, "What could that be? Do I really have a duty to myself and my family?"

Your family is the group we discussed in the first chapter. They are your mother, father, and siblings in your nuclear family; the uncles, aunts, and grandparents in your extended family; and the teachers, mentors, and coaches in the further extended family.

Marie and Sheldon: Single-parent household

Marie and Sheldon grew up with their mother, a single parent. They saw their dad about twice a year. They never knew where he lived, and from their mother's grumbling, they learned that he never gave their mom any financial or other support to nurture his children.

They vaguely remember any mention of his other family. This meant that perhaps they didn't meet a brother or sister who they never knew existed. Life at home was challenging. Mom worked long hours, and when she came home, she was always tired and running around to keep up with chores and to supervise homework. The children had to help with the chores, food shopping, and preparing meals. They never seemed to spend much time just hanging out or playing with friends.

Doug: Two-parent household

Doug lived with both his parents. His father was strict and his mother was soft spoken. His father was determined that he and his three brothers "toe the line." He monitored their every move. Whereas their mother would come home from work, fix a meal, and read in her favorite chair, their father checked their homework, questioned them about school, checked their clothes and their bags, gave them marching orders to do chores, and on weekends, took them to baseball practice and watched until they were done. He had spent several years in the Army and always had to be in control.

Matthew: Extended family

Matthew lived with his aunt and her husband. His father had been serving a sentence in jail since he was five years old, and his mother was always drunk. Custody was granted to his aunt and uncle, and although he was well taken care of, he felt lonely at times because he did not have any siblings or cousins around. He looked forward to school every day so he could see his friends and others closer to his own age.

The stories of immediate families are many and varied. Some children live with abuse and are always in need of love and material support. Some parents are loving and caring, some are strict, and some ignore their children because they are always busy.

Whatever the nature of the household, children have to contend with teachers and coaches of all different styles. The ideal would be for a child to grow up in a loving household and to be supported by loving and caring teachers and coaches.

It doesn't matter how you were brought up. All of these adults acted according to what they knew and believed. They felt they were doing the right thing. They grew up with similar influences in their childhood and faced their own issues. You may have been feeling the effect of their response to past experiences. It could be that you felt loved and secure because of their actions toward you or perhaps you suffered because of their action. Your perception of these incidences affected you then, and might even be affecting you now in the same way. Looking at a particular event, you might discover that you misunderstood their intentions.

When you leave the environment in which you were raised, you begin to learn that what worked for you then might not work now. You learn that some of what your parents and guardians did was for their benefit or for the benefit of onlookers. You also learn that many of the limitations you have now are a result of the experiences you faced in your early years.

When you are in your thirties, you begin to understand and see your own behavior or lack of achievement as resulting from the impact of your family's actions and your interpretations of them. It is not enough to know and understand this impact, however. To move forward and evolve into the great you, you must forgive. Any resentment, any regrets, any embarrassments, and any hurt must be removed from your thinking. To forgive doesn't mean to condone what your family did, but rather to free yourself from the effects of those actions. The Holy Bible says you should forgive seventy times seven times. Forgiveness is a process that has to be repeated every time you remember the offense. You are not letting them off the hook. You are freeing yourself to succeed. No one is worth that pain you go through.

It is important to forgive your family because their closeness amplified the biggest challenges you faced, and resentment does not necessarily heal with time. If carried over thirty, forty, or fifty years, you likely will develop issues related to these resentments. Conversely, forgiveness awakens us to the realization that, at the deepest level, we are one—in that we all are trying to make sense of our own journey called life. You should decide right now that you will not carry the effects of your family's past actions to your grave. No one is worth that. Let it go. Try to love your family members for who they are and for what you learned as a result of interacting with them. It is time to move forward.

4

WHAT DO YOU WANT?

This chapter looks at that frequently discussed topic of goals and examines how we should treat them. Everyone has goals, and for many people, these remain dreams and never are attained.

Let us visit our favorite place in the yard outside and mark off a section that we will use to develop our garden. This garden will have a variety of flowers. Some need shade, whereas others need the sun. Some need lots of water every day, and some just need a sprinkle now and then. They all have different rates of growth depending on the species, but we start all of them from the seed.

You would have to decide what you want to have in your garden. Obviously, you will decide on plants you like. You might decide what to grow based on the amount of care they require, the color of the flowers, and the height and size of the plants. The flowers will reflect you.

You will need to give them your attention with water and fertilizer. You will have to look out for any new weeds that appear. You also have to make sure the ground is ready and check on the drainage now and then. In other words, you have to focus and give this project your full attention.

Reaching your goals is one of the biggest desires you will have in life. One of the biggest disappointments you can experience is to reach forty and realize that you are nowhere closer to reaching your goals than you were decades ago. When you check the date on some notes you made on the day you set those goals, you may be surprised to know that ten years have passed and those goals remain but a wish. Does this sound familiar?

Maybe this is a good time to redefine your goals. These plans have to be drafted in relation to your uniqueness. You have a distinct combination of talents and a set of desires that are yours alone. The following activities can help you with this exercise:

- Assume that you have unlimited resources to handle the projects and write down a list of what you would like to accomplish.
- Write down a list of what you like to spend your time doing. Include smells, tastes, and sights that you like.
- Write down a list of things that wear you out, that you find boring, and that you don't like doing.
- Evaluate your list and identify what you see as the "vision" for your life.

Logic and societal rules tend to get in the way of our planning. So, we should write down these goals as if money were no object and the door of opportunity was wide open. Let us put logic and probability on the back porch for now.

Determine how you want to grow from the point at which you are right now. What are the skills and character traits you would like to have? You might want to be fit, firm, fabulous, and flexible. You might want to have special training in some area of expertise. You might want to be calm and able to cope in any situation, and you might want to make spiritual growth a priority in your daily life. Write this down.

Imagine a time when you would have acquired your special skills and ask yourself what you want to do with those skills. You might want to write books and blogs, conduct workshops, travel, make movies, be a board member of a large corporation, work from home, or spend lots of time with your family. This list can be as long as you want it to be.

Look next at some activities that are so fulfilling that they are worth far more than any money you could receive. Think of the ways the environment, or children, or a stranger, or a friend can benefit from your interest and your actions. This can be an activity that requires listening, spending time with someone, helping with transportation, or leading a prayer or support group as well as any others you can think of.

In devising goals, especially when starting out a life of your own, people tend to think only of money, a fine house, or the latest model car. Those might be desirable possessions, but their value tends to pale in comparison to those we just discussed. As you will come to see, life is so much more than achieving material goods and status, trying to impress others with glamour and glitter, and living a definition of success as suggested by the media. A goal that involves service and helping others is sustainable and self-fulfilling over the long haul.

You will ask yourself, "Why am I not pursuing my goals?" And when you evaluate your responses, you may have answered with any or all of the following reasons:

- You are surviving right now and don't see the need to put in extra effort to change things. The mediocre life is okay for now. At least you can pay your bills.
- You fear that friends and family might get uncomfortable with your progress. You hardly want to rock the boat.
- You feel guilty about the attention you give your goals in time away from your loved ones.
- You are afraid of being successful, and what it might mean in your circle of friends and acquaintances.

- Your dream is just a fantasy when you think of the probability of attaining such high ideals.
- You cannot see a clear path forward from where you are now to where you want to be.
- You simply don't know where to start.

During those years as an administrator of pension schemes, I remember speaking with people in their sixties who were going on retirement expressing regret that they had not dedicated their lives to their first love and passion. At sixty, no matter how much status you have acquired in business, no matter how much money you have accumulated, and no matter your material possessions, your soul will remain unsatisfied if you did not do what you truly loved. This revelation has stayed with me for years and it is one of the main reasons I chose to write this book.

Looking back in the garden, all those "ifs" and "buts" and fears are weeds that must be plucked and discarded. The garden that you construct is a manifestation of you, the individual. Even if you cannot identify a final goal, at least you know what you like to do. That is a start. Understand, too, that other people, even those close to you, might not see your vision. It is still your vision.

I think most people in their twenties, thirties, and forties understand this intellectually, but the problem is knowing how to achieve results.

Find two or three people dedicated to achieving their own goals. They don't have to see your vision or even believe in your dream. You don't have to see theirs, but you each can decide to share your results, set milestones along the way, and form accountability partners to whom you must report on a regular basis.

Make your goals your priority. Develop them daily. Act on them and refer to time markers along the way. Lack of action in this area is one of the biggest regrets you ever can experience. It is something you must do.

You are the only person who is guaranteed to be with you for the rest of your life and your action, now, is an investment in your satisfaction later.

5

SAY THE WORD! GET A LIFE!

There is a word that we have heard all our lives. As mentioned before, this word is used to teach us what is wrong, and so it keeps us on course, as we grow older. Let us look at how lives can be different because of the use or lack of use of this word.

Angie: Lazy coworker

Angie worked alongside Mira on projects in an office. Rather than do her own research, Mira always complained that she was having problems and Angie always helped her out, even if it meant staying an hour or two after work. What irritated Angie is that Mira would fast-forward her compilation and design covers and then boast to her boss and others that she was the first to complete the assignments.

Monty: Well-meaning spouse

Monty's friends invited him out for an evening at the jazz bar, but as soon as he reached home, his wife Marcia met him at the front door and, with excitement in her voice, announced that she had a surprise for his supper. To his horror, she made him lobster quiche. She knew that seafood definitely was not his favorite, worse yet, lobster. She had fixed those kinds of dishes in the past, and he plowed through them with great effort to avoid making her feel bad.

Some things simply irritate us. This irritation might be unique. Even when we were very young, we knew what went against our sense of comfort. Some things we didn't like, but we went along with the decision of the people in charge simply because they were bigger and more in control. We also may have feared what might happen to us if we didn't obey.

So now you are twenty-eight or thirty-four or forty-five, and guess what? You still are tolerating so many things in your life that you wish were different. You are pleasing everyone except yourself. It is not like you don't know what you want. You are just afraid to act. But what are you really afraid of? You are an adult now. No one is going to spank you or send you to stand in a corner, so why do you sabotage yourself?

I was guilty of tolerating things I didn't like. As a child, I hated milk. My father was employed at a milk-processing plant, and everyday he came home with a large bottle of milk that we were expected to consume, cream and all. All my childhood years, I went through this daily torture. As an adult, one day I asked myself, "Why am I still drinking this?" and I just kicked the habit.

We spoke about an important word earlier in this book. It is just one word, yet it speaks of a decision to walk a certain path. It can speak of a decision to finally let go of an issue. It can show people that they need to respect you because you know yourself and your intent to do what you want.

This word has only two letters, yet it makes a whole sentence. It conveys the exact meaning of a reaction. The word is no.

The lack of saying no is probably the reason you are involved in things or with people you don't care about. You decide not to use it "for a peaceful life." Once you experience an irritant, there is no such thing as a peaceful life. Everyone else might be smiling, but you are not. Can you keep on living this way? Do you even want to if you could?

When we were children, we ended up saying, "yes," when our hearts said, "no." It takes just two minutes for us to list those many times. As an experiment, select one time in your life when you wanted to say "no" but did otherwise. Look at how your life turned out. Now visualize what your life would have been like had you just said "no." In spite of all who you may have offended at the time, new and different opportunities would have presented themselves. Maybe we could find examples the other way around.

When you are in this privileged age group, you now are making decisions for yourself. You have to say "no" when that is what you want to say. Sometimes we would rather not say anything at all than say "no", but remember, not saying anything is giving consent and equates to saying "yes."

Practice pronouncing saying "no" in a sweet voice or loudly, in front of a mirror, or any of the many ways in which you can say "no." Try some of the following:

- "Thank you but I have made other arrangements."
- "Sorry, but I will not be a part of it."
- "This is not what I want for myself."
- "Sorry, but I am not available."
- "I do not agree."

..and we could list many more.

These examples could work for people who find it hard to say "no." They tend to bring an end to just about any request. You do not need to explain the details. This only weakens the impact of the response and opens the door to persuasion.

Sometimes not saying "no" can be an indication of indecision. It is the reason why we don't finally clean out that closet and give away those clothes we know that we definitely are not going to wear again. It is the reason our email boxes are cluttered: we procrastinate and will not just hit that "delete" button. Delete, and empty the trash.

People who are comfortable with "no" don't feel so much stress because they are at peace with their situation. People who fail to say "no" when they should, create an internal resistance and hence a resentment toward other people or themselves.

Now, you tell me: why would you sacrifice your well-being and peace of mind for the benefit of someone else? As the title of a book by Susan Jeffers says, "Feel the fear and do it anyway."

You will need this word for the rest of your life. Spell it, say it, and practice using it. Say it when you know you need to. Support it with your body language and don't send mixed messages. No!

6

YOUR BEST OCCUPATION

Now we will look at the activity called our "occupation." It is such a large part of our daily lives, and occupies so many years, that we could not discuss better ways of living without also looking at how we decide to best use our time, and what we expect from that decision.

Peter and Greg: Finding a job you love

Peter and Greg work in the same department of a chocolate factory. They report to the same supervisor and have identical job descriptions and identical working hours. They are required to work on appliances that are brought in for repair. Peter loves his job and can't wait to get to work in the mornings. It is just an organized way of doing what he used to do as a child. As a result, he is always upbeat and completes his tasks in record time. He loves his coworkers and has no intention of leaving this company, not in the foreseeable future.

Greg, on the other hand, drags himself to work every morning, complaining about something work related. He doesn't like what he is doing, and he hates having to get up early and rush through the morning traffic to drop off his wife at her job before getting to the factory on time. When he gets to his department, his mind is only on lunchtime or 5:00 p.m. when he finally can leave. He has no wish to be promoted or to stay with that company. He only accepted the job because he had been unemployed for a long time, the bills were piling up, and he was glad for the opening that had come up at this factory.

Who invented this thing called work, anyway? Are we expected to do the same thing for more than thirty years just to survive? Is that our total occupation?

You know yourself. You know what you like to do. What is that activity that you would do even if you never got paid to do it? You know the answer. The ideal situation is doing what you love to do and getting paid to do it. Then work becomes play.

Another thing to consider when choosing a career is lifestyle and individuality. Are you an early riser? Do you like a great social experience? Do like to be suited up or casual all day? Do you like being on the phone all day? Do you like quiet hours?

Your occupation should include your foremost desires. Not everyone can fall into an ideal work situation, so they might work only for the income and maybe the status. These people may plan to occupy themselves during their free time with what they love most.

The world has changed. It is good to know that more possibilities for work exist than ever before, and the amount of opportunities is multiplying daily. As discussed in Chapter 2, these possibilities are endless. You can expand your knowledge with courses to enhance what you already know. You can step into new fields. My next-door neighbor, after spending ten years teaching in a classroom, designed her own training program and now offers an online course from her living room. I know a guy named Owen who shed his jacket and tie and his lawyer's office to learn about and start a video editing service. It is easier than ever to shift into an entirely new field, to use social media to identify new employers, or even to design and develop your own business.

With all the platforms and applications available, you can use the templates and the guided instructions to create your own designs. The possibilities are endless. Given all the e-mail listservs and social media outlets, marketing is an absolute breeze, and even if you don't yet know how to market your business, numerous online courses are available on the subject.

We all are born creators, and we can use this faculty to design our careers. We can enjoy careers in more than one field, earning a monthly income, by the project, at weekend events, or passively to provide residual income. After all, who says we need to go to work at nine, stay there for eight hours, and keep this routine for life? Haven't we got options?

The fact is that we spend about an hour getting ready for work, perhaps two hours or more on our commute to and from work, and eight or nine hours actually working. That is approximately twelve hours a day. That is most of our waking hours. Isn't it totally reasonable for us to ensure that what we call "work" fits our preferred lifestyle?

If you are between twenty and forty years old, it is likely that you are working or are looking for a job. As you consider employment, try to enter a field of work that reflects you and your passions. And if a job you love currently is not available, plan to include time in your life for other outlets doing exactly what you love.

7

RELAX

"I now relax easily, and the more I relax, is the more relaxed I become".

"I now relax easily, and the more I relax, is the more relaxed I become".

Several years ago someone gave me the above affirmation, to repeat for relaxation. At the time, I didn't understand its usefulness, but now I am identifying relaxation as one of the secrets to a better life.

To relax is to lighten up, to ease, to make or become less tense or anxious. To understand how the subject of relaxation is a fundamental issue in the human journey, we would need to examine what it is, why do we need it, and what could happen if we don't practice it.

Tension tends to arise as a result of our dealing with daily challenges:

- To complete tasks
- To produce results quickly
- To compete
- To earn
- To satisfy others

Although we might not be conscious of it, we become tense when we hear bad news, when we feel resentment or when we worry about something that might happen.

A person will notice tightness in the shoulders and neck and ignore it until it becomes mental, emotional or physical discomfort. Tension disrupts the bodily functions and might be a prelude to physical ailments. In general, it is when the discomfort shows up as feelings of impending doom, panic attacks or unexplained nervousness that the victim shows up at the doctor's office.

It is reported that doctors are prescribing more anti-anxiety medication than ever before. Treatment may also include massage, and anxiety management programs to deal with on going problems. In these settings victims learn that the root of the problem lies in their perspective and, of course perspective arises from their core beliefs. This explains why two people encounter the same situation, yet they have different reactions.

The art of relaxation is essential. It reduces stress and reduces the things caused by stress. Consciously relax before you begin a task, after completing a task, before you pray, before you go to sleep. When I see how important it is to me, I wonder why it isn't taught to very young children. Brushing teeth is not the only essential skill.

There are a variety of techniques and coping mechanisms that may be applied when needed, such as:

- Sipping herbal teas
- Engaging in calming exercises

- Deep breathing
- Silence
- Affirmations
- A walk in natural surroundings

The method has to be what works for you as an individual, as you:

- Become aware of the need to relax in the moment
- Value yourself enough to know that something must be done
- Take action

Discover and practice an art that must be mastered to stay calm, poised and confident while you achieve more.

8

THE POWER OF A PROMISE

Everybody knows what a promise is. It is an assurance given to someone else that you definitely will do something. It creates an expectation in that other person that something definitely will happen.

So you might ask, "What does a promise have to do with choosing my best life? Is there something wrong with making promises?"

We have been hearing promises since we were children. These promises mainly were made to motivate us to get something done:

- "If you finish your homework, you will get to go out and play with your sister."
- "I will buy you a new pair of shoes if you keep your room tidy for a whole week."
- "If you do well at school this year, we can go on a trip for the holidays."

Then, there were the promises that were made without us having to do anything at all, such as the following:

- "When you get to the age of seventeen, I will buy you a car."
- "I will let you start music lessons next year."
- "I am going to bake your favorite cookies this evening."

The common thread in these examples is that we expected, and held accountable, another person to deliver on that promise. If it fell through, meaning that we did not get what was expected, we were disappointed. It might have even changed our opinion of that person, especially if it happened several times, and we became less hopeful in future instances.

In other cases, promises were not things to hope for because they actually were threats:

- "I am going to give away your favorite toys."
- "I am going to stop you from going to the playground on Saturdays."
- "I am going to report you to your teacher."

As we grew older, we too made promises and in bigger ways, and some of them ended up being formalized into contracts. If we examine this habit of ours, we might come to realize how much power a promise holds and understand that these promises can change the course of your life.

The contract you sign at your workplace is a promise. Other examples include entering into marriage or committed relationships; having children; accepting the post of club president; signing up for membership in a choir, band, or performing group; and agreeing to deliver goods or services on time.

We go about life making all kinds of promises to people. Some of them are easy to deliver, but many times we find ourselves overwhelmed, because we agreed to impossible deadlines, or we tried to do something without adequate resources. We also make lofty promises to ourselves, and even if we have the chance to change what we agreed to do, we stick with it simply because we made a promise.

So, are we to stay away from making promises? No. Rather, we need to be more aware of the different types and degrees of promises that can be made.

Ian and Sara: Degrees of commitment

Take a simple example. Ian is sick and his friend Sara is concerned. She could call him up and say, among other things:

- "Hi, Ian, I am calling to find out how you are. I will keep in touch."
- "Hi, Ian, I will stop by to see you sometime."
- "Hi, Ian, I definitely am coming to see you before the week is out."
- "Hi, Ian, I will pass by on my way home from work Monday or Tuesday."
- "Hi, Ian, I will stop by your place at lunchtime tomorrow."

Notice the different degrees of commitment in this example and that Sara is likely to be the person to choose which promise to make good on. Ian likely will be happy to see Sara whenever she decides to come by, or even just to hear from her. Sara needs to make the promise she can keep.

Some people live anxious lives because they have a habit of making promises that keep them bound and tied to unreasonable deadlines. This type of promise usually is made in an effort to please another person, and in many cases, it is not necessary. If you consider some of the repeated areas of stress in your life, you might find that they are related to unrealistic promises.

Weigh your future promises carefully. They hold power. Let them work for you, not against you.

9

WHEN YOU THINK YOU DON'T KNOW

We go through life constantly looking for answers to the questions that pop up at any given time. Some answers come right away, and others, in spite of asking again and again, we still don't have an answer. Sometimes, we get an answer to our question, but we don't recognize it as such, because it was not the kind of answer we were expecting.

The secret to finding answers is to ask. From Matthew 7:7-8 of The Holy Bible we read:

> Ask, and it will be given you;
> Search, and you will find;
> Knock, and the door will be opened for you.
> For everyone who asks receives,
> And everyone who searches finds,
> And for everyone who knocks, the door will be opened.

We all want to know how, why, when, where, and what. We want clarification to understand and look for assurance as to the best way forward. So, why don't we ask for help?

How many of us have been put down, for asking so-called stupid questions by friends, adults, schoolteachers, and even parents? Even now, we tend to feel some kind of hesitation whenever a question comes up. We might say to ourselves:

- I don't know what to ask.
- I don't know who to ask.
- I don't want anyone to be upset with me.
- I hate to feel stupid.
- I wonder what they will think of me.
- I just can't stand rejection.
- That person wouldn't know

The result of not asking, is having to work with only what we already know. We are not sure whether we are right, and we might spend time wondering about what to do, or we might give up on trying to know.

Alternatively, the result of asking means you know more. It can be a way to get what you want. It can help you sort out another person's intentions and can clarify assumptions. It enables accurate planning, and most of all, it makes you understand. The answer might be a simple "yes" or it might be a simple "no." Whatever answer you get to your question, life will go on.

Carol: An easy ask

Let us say Carol sees a lady with a hairstyle she really likes. She could go home and think about it, and then describe the style to a hairdresser who might not have a clue as to what she is suggesting, or she could go up to the lady, pay her a compliment, and ask her the name of her salon. Most likely, the lady would smile and be glad to tell her. Now, Carol can get her hair done, and can know she will like it.

Although it came a little late, I eventually learned that most people feel empowered when you ask them for help. It saves you time, it becomes a shortcut to getting what you want, and it helps you make connections with others.

You can find out what you want by asking one person. You also can find out what you want by asking in Yahoo! answers or Google or other search engines. Above all, people who practice prayer open themselves to receiving the right answers.

If you really want to live a better life, then you must begin to feel comfortable with asking empowering questions, such as "How can I get the job I truly love?" "How can I find a loving group of friends?" "What do I need to do next?" and many others. These questions move you toward open doors that can provide you with the results you need.

Instead of struggling so much, or settling for mediocrity, try to develop the habit of asking questions. As you watch the changes that result from receiving answers, you will get less and less afraid of asking, and as your confidence grows, so too will your success.

Ask and it will be given. The answer might come in unexpected ways, but it still comes. When you don't know, and your friends don't know, God knows. Just ask.

10

MOVE THAT OBSTACLE

Let's consider an all-too-familiar obstacle.

Ken: A standout guy

Ken is a bright, successful businessman, who became well known for his innovations and his ability to test uncharted waters, qualities that set him apart from his peers in the same industry. When not at work, he spends time in the company of his brother and two friends. He feels uncomfortable making new contacts, and is even afraid to get in touch with some people he already knows.

Lisa: A self-starter

Lisa resigned from her job as a graphic designer with a well-known marketing company, and decided to start her own business creating products for sale and supplying custom designs. She is concerned about her business, as she isn't able to get the volume she needs even though she has good contacts. Her problem is her reluctance to make the necessary calls, and to follow up on the proposals.

Tommy: A reluctant teen

Tommy is a teenager who would like to connect more with his classmates, but after every attempt, he second-guesses himself. He worries about what people say, and is fearful of taking the next step. As for inviting a girl out on a date, right now that is not in the cards.

Martin: A shy performer

Martin is an amazing stage performer, singing and dancing. But when the lights go out, and he is no longer on stage, he simply fades into the background of any scene and becomes anxious about approaching a stranger.

Many people can relate to one or more of the people just described. They are self-conscious, withdrawn, or timid, and these qualities may combine to form obstacles in their lives. These people are not necessarily introverts who are energized by being alone. Rather they want to interact with others, but the thought of it makes them uneasy. They are shy.

Shy people take longer to make a decision, going over the reasons for or against a course of action multiple times. They tend to procrastinate to delay having to deal with what they must do. Even after taking action, they may keep wondering whether they made the right decision and tend to worry about what others think.

The problem is that it is difficult for shy people to find their place in the world. It is the bold who know what they want, and go for it. They are not concerned with possible outcomes, and they do not fear rejection or competition.

If you are shy, you know it. I often hear people say, "I cannot sell anything" or "He owes me money, but I am not the kind of person who will call him about it." This makes you lose what you deserve. You allow people to be unfair to you. This way of living doesn't change itself and is an important behavior to change if you want to have a better life.

Your body language, timidity, and self-consciousness are revealed in your communication or noncommunication. People will begin to overlook you and take advantage of you based on what they see or don't see.

The question is, "How can you change this habit of yours?" Before you search for the answer, know that changing this behavior requires vigilance. Without a doubt, you are aware of the instances when you acted shy and, in hindsight, you might have resented your behavior. Think of what would have been a better way to act, and next time, decide to be bold. If you need to ask a question, ask it. If you need to claim what is yours, don't be like Lisa and shy away from opportunity. Instead, put yourself out there in order to get what you want. Take courage, and open up and talk to people you previously would have been reluctant to greet or confront. Your confidence will grow with practice.

Whether confronted with good or bad issues, bold people get what they want, not the shy. It is you who needs to fix this.

When working on the vision for your life, there is truly no place for shy people. Be bold.

11

THE VALUE OF FORMING HABITS

This chapter looks at the main habits of our lives that should help keep us grounded. These are places to which we can return when the going gets rough. These are places we always are assured of unconditional love and support, and from these connections, we receive balance and guidance toward solutions. These "places" can be people, physical spaces, music, food, reunions, books, exercise, worship, and anything else that grounds us.

The first step to staying grounded is to identify what keeps you in balance. The next step is to plan how to practice incorporating these things in our lives. The key task is to form a "habit." As a noun, it is—

- the application of an idea,
- the customary way of doing things and
- the act of doing something again and again to get better at it.

The following are some areas in your life for which you should develop a grounding practice.

Family

You are connected, by genes or by adoption, to the people you call "family." They are the facts in the story of your existence. Over the course of your life, you learn to be happy with, or in spite of, them. You learn to resolve conflicts, you see their mistakes, successes, and failures, and they mirror back to you many of your own issues. It is this closeness of interaction that makes the family a deep and special bond.

Whatever the nature of your family, you grow through the experience of being related to them.

You owe it to yourself to invest time and attention to your family members as a habit. This investment gives you and others a safe and soft place to fall when the need arises. As the years progress, the conflicts and the repeated differences of opinion give way to tolerance and love because that is what relationships are about.

Alone time

No matter how connected you may be, you need to plan for and practice alone time every day. Don't be like Tanya who is either at work or attending to family or picking up groceries or attending club meetings after work. Don't be like Ricky who stays involved in after-work projects and is always with his wife or his friends or the children.

Alone time is essential to reenergize your spirit, to pray or meditate, or to relax and take time to just inhale and exhale, with no responsibility and no interruptions. The impact of alone time is felt when you not only know about it but also practice it daily. You owe this time to yourself.

Invest your money

This habit of investing often is ignored when there are not enough resources to provide for expenses. Once you reach sixty years old, having calculated how much money you earned and the investments you've made to be comfortable financially, the habit of investing your money pays off big time.

Don't wait for a large inheritance, or sit back and wish for big wins from gaming.

Visit financial institutions, read books, and learn how investment instruments operate. Don't join the millions of people who regret not putting aside a small amount of money in regular installments. While you work you earn active income. Your goal should be to save and to set up a stream of passive income, which requires no additional work from you.

Spending is necessary, saving is good, but investing is essential.

Self-care

Eating right, exercising, carving out alone time, and taking care of your physical body all need to be practiced as a habit. Again, your quality of life is a result of what you practice. When you admire how well toned Marie's body is or how energetic Kenny always seems to be, you likely will learn that they have an exercise program and stick to it or that they carefully plan their meals.

Detox your life

"Detox" has become a buzz-word. Experts in health, especially in alternative therapies, constantly offer information about why we need to detox and the many ways it can be done. They also encourage us to detox with regularity. Some experts recommend once or twice a year, and others recommend various other periods of time. Simply walk into a health store and you will see bottles of liver cleanse, colon cleanse, kidney cleanse, blood cleanse, or even total body detox. They all are worth trying. Detox diets, detox programs, and detox workshops have become a big business.

So, why should anyone want to detox? The answer is that we all have toxins in our body. There can be no debate as to whether these toxins exist, but we tend to forget that toxins do not exist only in the body and in food but also in our minds.

On a daily basis, we are bombarded by the media, with stories of crime and violence with all the graphic display of the details. We are led to believe that conflicts can be resolved only by force. The movies are laced with themes of bad relationships, of people plotting to murder spouses, and of guns blazing.

Commercial ads try to convince you that you are not good enough. You need to lose weight, drive a better car, drink a special brand of alcohol, smoke, spend, and gamble. At the same time, you are told to "Eat this, to get that," try raw, gluten-free, vegan, or high-protein foods (but some people also say that too much protein damages your kidneys). The wellness industry generates confusion and fear.

The media also sensationalize politics and the economy at home and abroad in an attempt to keep the attention of viewers. In addition to the media, in everyday experiences, you meet Miss Chin, Mr. Green, and Mrs. Black who each have their own issues and are advising you about what to do. Friends and relatives also make you feel so drained every time you see them or hear their voices.

The fact, my friend, is that you are suffering from information overload, with opinions persuasively delivered that sometimes are far removed from what you are all about and with a value system that could be completely remote from who you are.

It is so important to identify the things that are toxic to our emotional peace and, every now and then, take a scheduled break from them and think freely. This detox advice is as relevant to our bodies as it is to our minds. Getting rid of information overload is an excellent way to keep our sanity.

These grounding behaviors have to be formed by the number one habit of practice. We cannot do it just today and not tomorrow, or else we never will reap the benefits. Be like some religious groups. Dedicate one day each week on which you never work. For twenty-four hours, unplug from all that is going on. You have to be vigilant in these areas and see your detox habit as an investment in your own well-being.

We know that many things should be done, but the only thing keeping us from achieving the result we want is that we did not practice. Take Homer who understands all of the maneuvers in playing football and how all the muscles work. He knows how to increase his running speed and how best to breathe, but he will not excel without practice. Look at Maureen who is an accomplished violinist. She didn't get to this level by reading about the violin, or by looking at it. She had to practice. These are just two examples of a principle that says that the results you are getting in your life now, come as a result of what you have or have not been practicing all along.

In these examples it is the habit, the practice, that will bring you back to yourself and keep you grounded. You get good at anything you practice. This is true for winners and for losers. Practice good habits and let it be true for you, too.

12

PLAY

Everybody needs to play.

Spend an evening in the park and just watch the children play. They shout and scream, they tumble, chase each other, eat ice cream, mess up their clothes, create games, and laugh at every thing. They seem to have no cares at all. They live just for these moments of fun and happiness.

It is through play that children develop social skills, focus, decision-making skills, and the ability to pretend and visualize, which all help them as they grow. They know how to have a good time.

Somewhere along our journey of life, the percentage of our playtime reduced, until, for some of us, it disappeared altogether. As we got caught up in preparation for school, or the desire to achieve in sports or in music lessons, we gradually let go of this carefree activity of play. Then came the rush for college credits, and the hope for a good grade-point average. Somewhere in our twenties, thirties, or forties, "play" fell off the to-do list. We forgot what it was, and we began to live like the adults we knew, and somehow, we just could not get back into the rhythm of play.

We get up early to fulfill a work agenda, we work after work, and we fill each free hour with any outstanding work.

Play is essential to the well-being of adults. It is the element that refines relationships, enhances creativity, and changes our perspective. It is letting go and enjoying the moment along a path that keeps us balanced and peaceful.

Lack of play has been identified as a possible contribution to criminal activity and a probable cause for many illnesses. Many books have been written about the healing power of play.

Jenna, an accountant, spends hours crunching numbers in her eight hours at work. She sometimes takes home projects and attends to them in the evenings and on weekends. The remaining hours of her weekend are spent doing household chores, watching television or reading a book. Marcus spends long hours running his highly successful business. His projects and appointments are carefully planned and executed. He does not schedule fun and play in his very detailed plans.

Because adults like Jenna and Marcus tend to feel guilty about playing, or see it as only an activity for competition, the closest they come to any form of play is to press "play" on the remote control.

The way to break the cycle is to increase and improve our human connections. They open up doors of opportunity. They keep us happy. Circulation has to be powered and maintained, so we have to keep our joints well oiled. Some people at seventy-five are more alive than others at forty. Aliveness has nothing to do with age.

So, as you go forward, improve your overall health and plan to play a game, watch a slapstick comedy, eat some ice cream, dance, and do anything that is fun. If that friend you invited to come with you doesn't want to go, call somebody else or go by yourself. Change your outlook, change your life, and play.

13

HELP SOMEBODY

This chapter is particularly special to me, and I am dedicating it to my mom who passed away one year before the time of writing.

My mom lived a full and exciting life as a teacher, and after early retirement, she was able to travel around the world with my dad on his business trips. Of my siblings, I was the closest to her geographically, and so in the last ten years of her life, we were able to discuss a number of issues relating to the many changes she was experiencing.

I asked her, "After living for ninety-two years, what single, most powerful advice would you give to myself or anyone else?"

Her reply was simple: "Help somebody."

From further discussion, I began to understand exactly what she meant.

We tend to get caught up trying to earn enough money to pay the bills and tending to our own family and our own little world that we hardly find it necessary to reach out to others.

Just look around and you will see that many people have needs. For some, it is financial need or some tangible offering, but most of the time, the need is for a sharing of a smile, two minutes of your time, or a listening ear. In that instant, it may seem like a bother, an extra effort, but just one simple act of kindness could ease someone else's burden. By uttering a single sentence, you could open a door for someone. You ask a few questions and give someone your undivided attention, and you might be easing pain that you did not know existed.

The greatest benefit of helping someone is that you learn what he or she learns, and more. By helping someone solve a problem and working through the steps with them, you have helped them rise to a better place and also have learned something along the way. The good you generate returns to you.

Margaret, my mom, was never hesitant to reach out to people, to encourage others, and to be a friend. Her students remember the little ways in which she made life better for them. She would smile at someone in the supermarket. She would remember to follow up earlier concerns with a phone call. She always felt that above all of her career achievements, her successes as a wife and mother, the enjoyment of her hobbies and her travels, the satisfaction of singing, and the pleasure of her friends that she was able to find the most peace and satisfaction from knowing that she made helping others a priority in her life.

When you help, you grow. Look around you and help somebody.

14

WHEN WHAT YOU THOUGHT WOULD BE, ISN'T

Rosie and Marie: Friends change

Rosie and Marie were best friends at school. They left for separate colleges in the same year, and after college Marie went to live in Malaysia where she did research and postgraduate studies. Rosie got married after college and settled in a beautiful home in her hometown.

Marie was planning to visit home for the Christmas holidays so she contacted her friend, and they agreed to meet for an evening out.

The restaurant was warm and inviting and the food was delicious. They chatted about all that had gone on in the interval of time since they last saw each other. Marie was now more into traveling, nightlife, and freedom. She had exciting stories to share with her friend. Although the meeting was pleasant, something made her feel a little uncomfortable.

Rosie's life was more about looking after her family, which now included two boys in a quiet complex where people were interested in backyard gardens, walks in the park, church, and PTA meetings.

She realized quite early on in this encounter that the two friends now had very little in common. It was not like the old days. From Rosie's perspective, Marie seemed a little "worldly," not only in what she talked about and how loudly she laughed, but also in what she wore and how she spoke to the waiter.

After spending three hours together catching up on old gossip and fond memories, they hugged and parted. Except for a few interactions on social media, that was the last time they met.

People change.

Larry: Family changes

Larry was on his way to see his mother. He had been traveling for four days. He had been stationed in the Middle East where he fulfilled his duties as an army doctor at several stations overseas. The last time he made this trip, he had come to his father's funeral.

When he arrived, the town and the house looked the same. People were still going about their Saturday chores, and children were playing in the same park he played as a child.

The atmosphere in his home was different, however. His mom was no longer the quiet, homemaker he remembered. She was glad to see him, but clearly she had many other interests that kept her busy. When she told him all about her new life and her exciting events, it was clear that his mom had changed.

Phil and Petra: Partners change

Phil and Petra had been married for ten years. They met at school and had been so close and couldn't wait to get married and to start a family. After seven years into the marriage, Petra let Phil know that she always had dreamed of being a singer, and although she loved her family, she knew it was time to study further and fulfill her heart's desire. The perfect college for training was far away from home.

Phil always knew of her desire, but he was happy with how things stood, and he also knew she enjoyed teaching dance at the prep school on Marley Avenue. He knew she enjoyed baking on weekends and reading bedtime stories to the children every night, but this declaration of hers came as a shocker. What would happen to the children? What would happen to him? Why the change?

Many people go through life not understanding that other people change. It is not that they lied when they made promises years back. It is not that they have become monsters overnight. Most likely, you will agree that you, too, have changed.

I saw an episode of the television show Where Are They Now? in which a rock star left the stage one night and just said, "I cannot do this anymore." He decided to give up stardom and got involved in church, and he became a happy family man. I know of a girl, Alyson, who grew up in a rural village. When she left for college, she told her family that she never was coming back to live a boring country life.

Why do people change?

People change because they need to. Some people grow, and some remain as they were twenty years ago. Who a person becomes is usually a calling from the soul and might have nothing to do with you or anything you did. All people, especially those in their late thirties, will one day look at their lives and ask themselves a big question: "Is this what I wanted out of life?" Sometimes, after lots of effort, the old ideals just do not work anymore. Sometimes, other people stay the same and you change.

So, what is the answer, and what are the options?

If your answer to "Is this what I wanted?" is "yes," then you have nothing to worry about.

If your answer is "no," then you need to decide whether to continue living as you are to avoid hurting someone else, or to follow your heart and find a new life that makes you happy.

Your parents might suddenly have a different attitude to that when you were growing up. Your enemy might become your friend, your closest acquaintance might change, or you might change. You might bring on your own suffering because you want things to be permanent when they are not. Sometimes change in a relationship (whether friend, family, or partner) is hard to accept, but somewhere along the journey, you need to accept that people change.

Look out for it.

15

ONE LAST QUESTION

It is said that if you watch six-year-olds occupy themselves and what they take an interest in, you will have an idea of what their calling might be. If we look closely, we see little doctors, artists, performers, teachers, and cooks. Later, we wonder where did the child in us go?

Well, it is the focus away from ourselves into hard work to make money and to get things done that makes us forget our inner child and what he or she truly loved. It is the influence from society as to how success is defined that keep us on a roll, maybe one that does not suit us.

You enjoy some things so much that you would do them whether or not you were paid. These activities can keep you occupied for hours on end. As a child, you would find pure joy in the act of creating and couldn't wait to get out of bed every morning to get going.

You need to list those things and do them. You can either do them for employment, in which case work becomes play, or you can carve out the time you need to do them in addition to your regular job. What is most important is that you live your passion and honor your calling to make your life better as well as the lives of those around you.

Write down the top five things you enjoy doing. How many times have you done each of these things in the past month? Very few, I suspect.

Sometimes it is difficult to get around to doing what you need to do. I know that all too well. The way to get around this problem is to enlist a friend or relative to hold you accountable (see Chapter 4). If you like to dance, it makes no sense to dance alone in front of a video in your living room. One day you will just stop. It is much better to enroll in a dance program. Learn salsa or hip-hop or whatever your favorite style of dance. The songs, the beat, and the energy of people with similar interests will give you the zeal to stick with the program.

If you love working with children, then you either should train to be an early childhood educator in which case you will be seeing and working with children all day, or volunteer to work at a children's home or teach Sunday School.

If you like the beach, schedule regular visits to the beach. If you like being with friends, find ways to connect with them often. For the things you must do, like exercising, you have so many options available. Dance, swim, run, or exercise at the gym. The more you keep doing what you enjoy, the healthier you will be.

You are who you are and you either can resist all your life or you can discover the joy of being you. Let your partners, your parents, your friends, and your children know that living your dream is your priority and stand firm.

You are the only one who is sure to be with you for the rest of your life. The number one secret is to embrace what we expressed in Chapter 1. This is your life.

In your final moments, you will reflect on your life, the people you met, and the goals you accomplished. You will remember how you overcame failures, how you changed paths, and where you found answers to the many things you wondered about. Many things that you were anxious about will have faded into the background, and material goals might not even seem to be important, but one question you are bound to ask is, "How would I like to be remembered?"

The goal of finding fulfillment guides you to learn much about yourself and your world and then ushers you into a better life.

16

RESPONSES

This chapter summarizes the responses to each of the questions posed to a number of people evenly spread across the twenties through forties. I taught in high school for several years and directed performing groups, so I decided to make contact with some of them and they, in turn, referred me to some of their friends. I included a few strangers in the group. The answers are listed below:

1. *What do you love most about your life now?*

Twenty and early thirty year olds spoke of:

- Freedom
- Excitement of possibilities
- Independence
- Enough time to make mistakes
- Being glad to be able to make his or her own decisions.

Older respondents:

- Felt wiser
- Felt more in control

- Felt fulfilled
- Did not care much for what people thought of them.

2. *If you had the chance to relive your childhood up to age sixteen, what would you have done differently?*

There were a variety of responses across the age groups such as:

- They would have learned to play an instrument or been involved in the arts and sports
- They would have paid more attention to studies
- They would have chosen different school subjects
- They would have been bolder and would have explored more options

3. *What are your best childhood memories under ten years old?*

The following were mentioned across all ages:

- Family outings
- Playing with friends
- Visits to grandma
- Summer holidays.

Two respondents said they would not wish to relive their childhood.

4. *Looking ahead, what are your concerns?*

The twenty year olds were concerned mainly about:

- Settling into relationships
- Taking on responsibilities

The thirty and forty year olds named finances as their number one concern, whether they would be able to cope.

Forty year olds were concerned about finances and the challenges of aging.

5. *Are you satisfied with your career choice?*

About seventy percent were satisfied with their career. The rest were glad for the income but would prefer to be working regularly in some other field.

6. *Do you think you have enough fun in your life?*

All twenty year olds felt that they had enough fun. About half of the thirty and forty years olds felt that they would love to have more fun.

7. *Do you find some of your beliefs lacking or unfulfilling?*

Almost all the twenty years olds were satisfied with their beliefs and the general rules that guided their life. Those over thirty questioned some of their beliefs, and had to do some adjustments in their life in order to cope.

8. *What questions do you have about life?*

The following questions were mentioned across the age groups:

- What is the use of working so hard?
- Why do people suffer?
- Why are there inequalities across gender?
- What is the point of trying to succeed, to study, and to earn if you are going to die?

9. *What are the things in life you don't love, but that you have to accept?*

Twenty year olds listed:

- Disappointment
- Failure

Most of the thirty year olds mentioned:

- Work
- Routines
- Taxes
- Sickness
- Death

Older respondents cited:

- Racism
- Classism
- Disregard of human life
- Death

10. What do you think is your life purpose?

Twenty year olds saw their purpose as:

- Making people happy
- Making medical breakthroughs
- Changing lives
- Entertaining.

About twenty percent of the older respondents felt that their purpose is to help people in some way while the remainder said they are still trying to find their life purpose.

11. What advice about life would you give to someone age fifteen?

The following were the responses across all ages:

- Don't be so afraid
- Stop worrying about trying to fit in
- Decide on what you love and go for it
- Explore

- Work hard for what you want
- Listen to your mentors

12. *What makes you truly happy?*

The twenty and some of the early thirties responded:

- Party time
- Outings with friends
- Family time

The others up to late forties responded:

- Having enough money to pay the bills
- Spending time with children
- Living my authentic self
- Helping someone feel better

13. *If you were to choose one cause that you feel strongly about, what would it be?*

The following were listed in all age groups:

- Poverty and hunger
- Abuse of women and children
- Child neglect
- Attainment of world peace
- Education as lifelong learning

14. *Do you worry about disasters? illness?*

Those who admitted to worrying about disasters listed terrorism, war and political upheaval.

Those who admitted to worrying about illness were in the late thirties or in their forties.

15. What is it that you see in people over 60 years old that you fear most?

Twenty year olds responded:

- Being dependent
- Financial instability
- Illness
- Becoming miserable

Twenty eight to forty two year olds responded:

- Insufficient funds for retirement
- Loneliness
- Working for another thirty years
- Being unfulfilled
- Health challenges

Responses from ages up to forty-nine were:

- Loneliness
- Physical challenges, weakness
- Inactivity
- Insufficient funds
- General deterioration in quality of life

Summary of observations

All of the respondents enjoyed the freedom of not being a child anymore and the endless possibilities that life can offer. A consistent response was appreciation for "Fun times with family and friends in the early years." A few respondents also mentioned sad memories of childhood.

As people get older, they begin to regret not having taken more risks, or not having been involved in creative ventures and the arts, and the occasions for having fun seem to get less and less. They begin to question some of the beliefs they hold about what is right for them and how to decide.

Respondents in their late thirties and forties are glad for the authority and wisdom they seem to gain as they age. They embrace the value of taking care of themselves in the areas of nutrition and fitness, and they pay attention to service to others and the "whys" of life as they also express concern about coping and spiritual growth.

In general, most people are happy with their choice of occupation, although the older respondents saw the need to include more of what they liked in their routines. Interestingly, respondents didn't seem to worry about physical disasters or physical security, but financial failure, relationship failures, and issues of aging were among the most significant fears.

17

WHAT NOW?

Balance

We all have been programmed, and our lives have been created from wishes and desires we inherited from other people. Establish your own rituals. Determine the combination of factors that create stability for you, and the frequency (weekly, monthly, annually) that you need to maintain this stability. Determine what motivates you, and make it a habit to reward yourself.

Independence

We are in a society, and its members are somewhat interdependent. Whether you live, work, worship, or play alone or in a group, you have to find a degree of independence that will give you the life you want that reflects who you truly are. Stepping into this life is not as difficult as you think, and it enhances the quality of your relationships.

Survival

It is no secret that life presents us with challenges and changes. It is our ability to work through these issues and adapt that determines our success. This is when we need to don our creative cap and find solutions. Pray and ask. Nothing is impossible. Survival comes from not only what you know but also what you are prepared to learn. Be prepared to change. When you walk through a storm, you know some things for sure. You discover strength and courage along the way, and your future is better for it.

What is the message?

The messages in this book are found in the chapter titles. This message is about taking full responsibility for your life. Be the cause. Declare yourself capable and step into action. Pray for "zeal," the quality that energizes you to complete any task. You might think you know all about the ideas presented in this book, but you still need to find the one thing that spurs you into action. This tendency to wait on someone to change, to wait for someone to give you the job you want, to wait on the good things you deserve to fall from the sky diminishes the quality of your existence while you are here on earth. Find out what works for you. Examine your mask of goodness and morality, education, and culture. Who knows? You might need to make some adjustments.

When you tell the truth, you open up your world and inspire others to do likewise. This book holds a message of letting go of the satisfaction you feel in mediocrity, changing the promises you made to yourself and others, and walking into a life of meaning, happiness, and service. What you don't fix at twenty, or thirty or forty, will be waiting to be fixed at sixty.

Now is the time to take full responsibility for your future. As the author of your life story, you can now choose to rewrite your script.